CW00494336

THIS HOUSE NAMED BURRSWOOD

By the same author:
DOROTHY KERIN: UNE VIE UN SIGNE
in collaboration with the Rev. G. Grosjean (Geofranc)
THE CHURCH OF CHRIST THE HEALER
THE TEACHING OF DOROTHY KERIN
THE LIFE OF DOROTHY KERIN
DOROTHY KERIN 1889-1963 - Her Ministry of Healing

Burrswood 1948. By courtesy of the artist S. Geoffrey Kendall.

THIS HOUSE
NAMED BURRSWOOD

By

Foreword by

The Right Revd John Perry
Chairman of the Board of Trustees, Burrswood
1989-2003

THIS HOUSE NAMED BURRSWOOD

First Published in 1989
New Edition 2008

Johanna Ernest

Published by
The Dorothy Kerin Trust
Burrswood, Groombridge, Tunbridge Wells, Kent. TN3 9PY

ALL PROCEEDS FROM THE SALES OF THIS BOOK WILL SUPPORT THE WORK OF THE DOROTHY KERIN TRUST

Reg charity number 1095940

Printed by CK Litho, Unit 3 Enterprise Centre
Chapman Way, Tunbridge Wells, Kent. TN2 3EF

Except the Lord build the house,
they labour in vain that build it.
Psalm 127

Contents

Illustrations

FOREWORD

The decision to re-print *'This House named Burrswood'* after a long gap will be widely welcomed. Memories can be short and recollections confused. Johanna Ernest comes to the rescue by providing a fascinating historical context for Burrswood, stretching back to the 18th Century. For example, she describes how one of the previous owners, Sir David Salomons, had the house rebuilt between 1834 and 1838, and ensured that the Jewish *mezuzah* - a symbol of hospitality and brotherly love - was incorporated into the stonework near the front door. A foretaste of God's future destiny for Burrswood as a House of hospitality, hope and healing!

We also learn that Burrswood was up for auction in 1948 - much the worse for wear after being requisitioned by the Army during the 2nd World War. It looked even more derelict on a day of relentless rain, when Dorothy Kerin went to view it. Yet, as she wrote later: 'As soon as I arrived on the door-step I felt sure that this was the house...it was dilapidated, but I seemed to see it as it could be - something beautiful for God to use'. So it has proved. Restored buildings matched by restored lives.

Over the years, the name of Burrswood has become synonymous with a holistic understanding of the ministry of healing. Countless people have passed through its doors and discovered, in their varied needs, that medicine and ministry are seen as one in the expert treatment, nursing care, prayer and counsel that are provided. God is concerned for the whole person.

In an increasingly impersonal and damaged society, places

of refuge and restoration are in short supply. The House named Burrswood shines as a beacon of hope; a safe place where acceptance and healing are gladly offered in the name of Jesus. It stands, too, as a challenge and encouragement to the Church in each local community to hold and share that same transforming vision - the Good News of the Kingdom of God.

Rt Rev John Perry

Former Bishop of Chelmsford
Chairman, Burrswood Trustees (1989-2003)

Acknowledgements

Sincere and grateful acknowledgement is made to all who have given generously of time and thought to the preparation of This House Named Burrswood; the Rt Revd John Perry, former Bishop of Chelmsford and past Chairman of the Trustees of Burrswood; to John Waldegrave Head, M. A. (Cantab.) , F. I. M. A. , for reading the first edition of the book in typescript; to Mrs Barbara Lee for her generosity in allowing extracts to be taken from her publications; to Marnie Bassett whose invaluable researches enabled much of past centuries to be remembered; to S. Geoffrey Kendall for his drawing of Burrswood 1948; to Victor Roberts for his sketch of the coach house; to J. M. C. Wheeler, M.B.E., F.R.S.A., Hon. Curator, The David Salomons Collection, for the photographs of the coach used by David Salomons, and the first house of Burrswood, and for his unfailing help with the period devoted to David Salomons; to the late Sir Victor Windeyer for his letter 14th April 1987, from Australia; to the Administrator, National Trust, Victoria, Australia; to Charles William Johnstone for his memories of Burrswood; to the Executive Director of the Jewish Welfare Board for permission to re-print the prayer of Emma Abigail Salomons; to Professor Raphael Loewe, and Mr E. Godfrey, for their detailed information about the blessing of a Jewish home; to Miss J. Mauldon, the Reference Librarian, The County Library, Tunbridge Wells; and the archivists and librarians of the following libraries - The British

Architectural Library, The Association of British Architects, The Victoria and Albert Museum, The Bodleian Library, The British Library, and to the Rector of Speldhurst Parish Church for his kindness in researching through the Church Registers. And finally grateful thanks are accorded to the many people who have made known details of former years, which have assisted in building up this presentation of the history of *This House Named Burrswood.*

Chronology

Initially the land belonged to Groombridge Place.

1734	Mortgaged estate vested in Chancery.
1754	Bought out of Chancery by William Camfield.
1781	Estate divided between two of the five sons of William Camfield. John Camfield remained at Groombridge Place. Henry Camfield lived on Burrswood Estate. It is probable the first 'Burrswood' described as 'a modern farm house' was built by Henry Camfield. His descendants continued to live there till 1831.
1832-52	Sir David Salomons J.P.
1870-end of century	Sir Walter George Stirling Bart, J.P.
1887	The Grand Duke Mikhail Nikolaievitch.
1906-18	Edwin James Johnstone.
1919	Mrs Johnstone.
1927-37	Sir Derrick William Inglefield Watson, Bart.
1939-45	Occupied by Army.
1945-48	Untenanted.
1948-63	Miss Dorothy Kerin.
1963-69	The Public Trustee.
1963	The Dorothy Kerin Trust. The First Trustees. The Diocesan Bishop of Rochester. The Lord Bishop of Coventry (Chairman). The Suffragan Bishop of Tonbridge. Edward Aubert M.D. (Warden of Burrswood). And others.

Introduction

This House Named Burrswood received the name from the nature of the land upon which was built the first house, during the latter part of the eighteenth century. This was termed a modern farm house. The present house of this name was built for David Salomons, a liveryman of the Coopers Company, between 1834 and 1838. The architect was Decimus Burton.[(i)] It shows the developing interest in the gabled Elizabethan style, the garden front combining four gables, only the detail giving an asymmetrical touch, while the entrance is unashamedly romantically asymmetrical.[(ii)] The cottage, about three-quarters of a mile on the right of the ascending path which leads from the village green, is dated about 1646. This was probably the first habitation built upon this piece of waste land. Initially it was two cottages, the homes of farm labourers, employed at Groombridge Place. Later this cottage became the coachman's house, when the stables, two cottages and a coach house, together with a harness room and a building for the storage of apples, were added to the property for David Salomons, behind which was a walled vegetable garden. The cottage was restored in the early nineteen seventies, when the front wall gave way, without warning, during one night. Before the land known as Burrswood was cultivated, the name was spelt with one R. It was indeed a bur wood, a wood of tangled undergrowth and innumerable springs with clear water.

(i) Decimus Burton 1800-81.

(ii) *Guide to Exhibition of the work of Decimus Burton,* Philip Miller, 1981.

Before continuing with the history of Burrswood, it might be rewarding to consider another word in the title *'This House Named Burrswood'*. The word house signifies a place within which to dwell, as well as the household, or persons living in the house; it can include also kindred and lineage. Indeed the Church is alluded to as the house of God. From the moment of research into the history of this house, attention is riveted upon this wider, more embracing aspect. Throughout the centuries the love of God, revealed through love for the neighbour, whether man or beast, together with a responsibility towards every form of nature, has been paramount in spite of the changes in ownership. Even the smugglers,[(i)] who were rife in Kent and Sussex during the early part of the eighteenth century, seem to have been on friendly terms with the villagers, who enjoyed the luxuries from their illegal activities. Each of the two fields in which these transactions took place, retained the name of 'brandy field',[(ii)] for decades after trading had ceased.

The actual stone buildings have been reshaped, and re-adapted to meet the changing needs of each decade. For many centuries the name of the bur wood referred to an area of dense woodland, practically a wasteland. For centuries it was probably passed by, unnoticed, by armies invading or retreating, across the small bridge which divides Kent from Sussex, and which must be crossed either way, to enter or leave the county at this point, on account of the River Medway, and the expanse of water before Groombridge Place, and at the entrance to the path which ascends to Burrswood. The name of Burrswood is also symbolic. It symbolises the confusion in the mind of man, who is forever seeking his true identity, and the reason for his being.

(i) John Bowra. Born in Groombridge 1713. A smuggler who became a cartographer.

(ii) Tithe map 1841. Also auction notice 1832.

INTRODUCTION

The burden which beset the mind of Christian is no less a burden in the mind of man today.

As I walked through the wilderness of this world, I lighted on a certain place where was a den, and I laid me down in that place to sleep; and as I slept, I dreamed a dream. I dreamed, and behold I saw a man clothed in rags standing in a certain place, with his face from his own house, a book in his hand, and a great burden upon his back. I looked and I saw him open the book, and read therein; and as he read he wept and trembled; and not being able longer to contain, he brake out with a lamentable cry, saying, 'What shall I do?'[(i)]

(i) *The Pilgrim's Progress*, John Bunyan, 1678.

William Camfield

Above the porch of the Church of St John, the Evangelist, Groombridge, is a stone upon which is inscribed the name of William Camfield. The date 17 is clear, but the further numerals are almost erased by the crumbling stone. The date is probably 1757. Beneath this is carved a sentence in Latin;

> OB FOELICISSIMUM CAROLI PRINCIPES EX
> HISPANIA REDITUM SACELLUM HOC.
> DOM 1625. I.P.

This inscription commemorates the return from Spain of Prince Charles, not betrothed to the Infanta Maria.

The Church, previously alluded to as a chapel, was built in A.D. 1625 by John Packer, a devout official at the court of King James. John Packer owned the estate of Groombridge Place to which belonged the acres of land upon which the house named Burrswood stands today.

Nearly thirteen decades of intense historical significance separate the two inscriptions on the stone above the porch; and the name above the Latin inscription should have had second place.

Almost one hundred and forty years stand between the two records to be remembered, but does it matter? The historic past is like this. Names and dates become intermingled. Momentous happenings are subdued in retrospect. Measured time has no lasting substance. It is the result of each event, and its significance for the future, which has importance. Had Charles married the Infanta of Spain, history might have been different, but to whose advantage no one can say. People were weary of the continued threats of war and an impending invasion by Spain throughout the reign of Elizabeth I. This borderland of Kent had suffered too many invasions already. The subsequent marriage of Charles to the zealous French Romanist, Henrietta Maria, is not part of this narrative, yet a passing reflection on the subsequent renewed religious conflict endured by the people of England, made this moment of rejoicing and thanksgiving of short duration. The death of James I in 1625, and the Civil War in 1642, did not bring the years of peace for which the ordinary people had been hoping.

Four generations of the Packer family had owned the Manor of Groombridge between 1616 and 1734. The last male member of the Groombridge branch of the family had died in 1709. The fortunes of the family changed, and by 1734, the mortgaged estate became vested in Chancery. The village of Groombridge might well have fallen into ruin and obscurity.

What might have influenced William Camfield, a wealthy yeoman, living in the parish of Speldhurst, to buy the estate out of Chancery in 1754? The estate, which was in a state of neglect and disrepair in 1734, would have been derelict by this time, twenty years later. This is a question which must remain unanswered for ever. Yet the answer may have been the same one which had motivated Abraham and the prophets, and many unrecorded people, to respond to a deep inner conviction, or who just knew within themselves they must act in a certain manner which would be contrary to their established mode of life. Whatever was the initial motivation, William Camfield, a man of true and simple faith, a tanner and currier, and a welder of iron, took up residence in Groombridge Place in 1757, together with his wife and five sons.

In 1766, a journeyman - bookseller, who kept a meticulous

diary of important events, recorded . . . 'William Camfield, the present proprietor who has with indefatiguable application and great expense *(sic)* retrieved the mansion house, the chapel and the whole village from the most ruinous condition that can be conceived and made it an agreeable and thriving place, in which his generous public spirit must ever be remembered with gratitude'[(i)]

William Camfield died in 1781. His son, John, lived at Groombridge Place until his death in 1788. Henry Camfield inherited Burrswood, and his descendants continued to live there until 1831.

(i) *Groombridge Place*, Barbara Lee, 1979.

Henry Camfield

Henry Camfield was born at Burrswood on 26th June 1799, the son of William and Ann Camfield, and the great grandson of William Camfield, who had taken Groombridge out of Chancery in 1754. He was baptized on 13th August 1799, in the Parish Church of Speldhurst. During the next few years his brother, William, and his four sisters were born at Burrswood: Eliza (Bessie), Maria, Matilda Susannah, and Ann. The registers of the Parish Church of Speldhurst are a testimony to the Christian family of Camfield who lived and died within the precinct of this historic Church, which was founded probably around the year 1200. This Christian family had received the principles of Christianity through the teaching, centuries before, of Theodore of Tarsus who would have been nurtured by the Church founded by Paul when he returned to his birthplace, after his direct encounter with the living Lord, upon the road to Damascus. And the faith that they had received stood firm during the centuries of political and theological unrest to which the country, and even the little villages, had been subjected. Henry Camfield grew up at Burrswood, and became both a tanner, and a welder of iron, as had been his forebears. He loved dearly the little modern farm house, which was his home, set among hop gardens, orchards, and fields, beside the stream, a tributary of the river Medway. His subsequent letters home from Australia bear testimony to an idyllic childhood.

Henry's father, William Camfield, was well aware of the difficulties in making a reasonable living from farming during the troubled times through which the country was passing. The years of the Civil War had caused a depression which had reduced farmers, and their agricultural labourers, to abject poverty.

Australia (New Holland) was in a state of colonisation. This was the time between the convict era and the discovery of gold. During May 1829, the following notice appeared in *The Times:*

> For the New Settlement at Swan River, and will touch at Rio Janeiro, the fast sailing and newly coppered poop ship Caroline Al burden 400 tons armed and with carriage guns. This vessel has very superior accommodation for passengers having seven feet between decks. The whole of the vessel being newly engaged, each person who may wish to avail themselves of this conveyance are requested to make an early application to James Henty Esq., West Tarring, Worthing, or 5 Arundel Street, Strand.

Henry Camfield applied to join this expedition, and so began a lasting friendship between these two families, the Camfields of Burrswood, and the Hentys, who had farmed in Sussex since the 14th century. On the 2nd June 1829, the *Caroline* sailed out of St Katharine's Dock, London, newly opened on 25th May 1828 for sailing ships. It is probable that Henry Camfield travelled to London, to join the ship, on the Brighton-London Stage Coach which stopped to change horses at the Crown Inn, across the village green onto which opened the gates leading to Burrswood. This coach continued to Tunbridge Wells, from where it departed daily at 9 a.m. and 4 p.m. The journey took five hours. William Camfield, Henry's father, may have taken the coach at the Crown Inn travelling in the opposite direction. This coach left Tunbridge Wells each afternoon and stopped at the Crown Inn, on the way to Brighton, where the journey terminated at the Blue Coach Offices.

From there William would have taken another coach to Littlehampton, to await the arrival of the *Caroline*, and to see his son for the last time. Two farm labourers, and their wives and children, may also have travelled this way, to embark later. They came from Speldhurst. Their most valued possessions, their farm animals, will have travelled with them. The *Caroline* was sighted off Worthing on 4th June, and anchored six miles out from Littlehampton next morning. Finally the labourers and their animals, as well as feeding stuffs, were taken on board, and the *Caroline* was carried away steadily, borne by a north-east wind, under a grey sky.

Rio Janeiro was reached on 26th July and on 12th October the West Coast of Australia was sighted. But the hazardous journey to the mouth of the Swan River had yet to come.

Henry's first letter home to Burrswood, left Fremantle during November 1829, and arrived at Penzance the following May, 1830. From there the letter made its way by galloping mail coach and was delivered finally on horse back, at Burrswood. The reply, written by his sister Maria, reached Henry during the following September.

Australia

The Swan River proved to be stark and uninviting when Henry Camfield disembarked from the *Caroline*. The grazing land was poor for the animals which he and James Henty had tended throughout the distressing voyage. Nevertheless he and James had formed a lasting friendship based upon the integrity of two men of sincere faith. To both these men their religious faith in God was the fundamental basis of their lives. Henry Camfield could not live without the help of God, and prayer was an inseparable part of his daily life. He went back and forth to God with all the problems with which his life was beset.

Immediately upon landing, James and Henry sought the Governor, Sir James Stirling. Captain Stirling had set sail in the *Success* in January 1827, to see for himself the conditions on the Swan River. He returned to London and, by his sincerity and his persistence, induced the British Government to agree to allow him to plant a Union Jack on the West Coast of the continent before the French took similar action. He returned to Australia on 17th January 1829, and on the 2nd May he hoisted the British flag in the name of George IV. His departure had been cited in *The Times*.

Henry Camfield and James Henty were given a grant of land, but from that time onwards a charge was made. As soon as he was established on his land, Henry built himself a dwelling of wattle and daub, and to link the past with the present he named his home Burrswood, after his Kentish home. It seems as if from now on, till the time of his death in

1888, that Henry lived on the memories of his former home, yet it is from these recorded memories that a picture of Burrswood in the 19th century can be envisaged. On the occasion of the wedding of James to Charlotte Carter she handed him a packet which she had brought from England. On opening it Henry found a pencil sketch of Burrswood drawn by his brother William. He became so lost in the enjoyment of this nostalgic bitter-sweet feast from his former home, on the other side of the world, that he forgot to tell his sister Maria about the wedding, when he wrote home. There was the fence at the bottom of the meadow, the oak tree where he had often lain in haying time, the spruce, the box tree, and the leaning fir, Pan's garden, and the ha-ha fence ... (i) Since the departure of the *Caroline*, the families of Camfield and Henty had seen each other frequently. Edward Henty and his sister Jane became regular visitors at Burrswood, and the same enchantment which had remained with Henry Camfield seemed to embrace Edward Henty. In 1831, Mr Henty senior, with his four sons, and his entire family, except for his son William, sailed to Australia in the *Forth of Alloway*. Edward Henty became a successful farmer, and he is acclaimed to have been Victoria's first permanent settler. He became a member of the State's Legislative Assembly. In search of land for grazing purposes, he established Victoria's first permanent settlement on the 19th January 1834. On this journey he was accompanied by Henry Camfield. In 1853 he built himself a house on a site overlooking Portland Bay. This house is looked upon as the most important early mansion house in Western Australia. He lived in this home for seventeen years. The name of the house is Burrswood. It was built from the locally quarried bluestone and featured in the 1984

(i) Many archives treasure the letters of Henry Camfield and the Henty family; their adventures and deprivations are told simply, by people who did not realise that they were heroes.

celebrations to mark the 150th anniversary of the Henty Settlement in Victoria.

On the momentous expedition of 1834 to explore Western Australia it may well be that Henry helped to choose the name of Edward's home as they stood together on the site upon which the house would stand in the years to come. Burswood[(i)] was built as a single storey mansion, in the Australian regency style, and it became the house to which the families, who had formed a lasting friendship came together whenever they could; these men and women who had shared the hazards of sailing upon uncharted seas in great ships entirely dependent upon the wind and the waves seeking for uncharted land. These were men and women who had adhered to their deep Christian principles with an unswerving faith, in every kind of danger, or personal hardship. And they enjoyed being together at Bur(r)swood and to share their memories of another home, on the border of Kent with Sussex.

(i) Burrswood is now, in 1984, spelt with one 'r', Burswood.

(ii) Architect John Barrow of Adelaide.

The End of an Era

Burrswood, Groombridge, was sold by auction on Thursday, 30th August 1832. The auction was conducted by a Mr Shuttleworth, at the Mart, Bartholomew Lane, opposite to the Bank of England, at 12 noon, in two lots.

> The 357 acres of superior land in high cultivation presenting from a finely undulated surface many delightful Sites for the erection of a Residence suitable to a Domain esteemed for its Romantic and highly Picturesque Character; twenty two acres of orchards and hop grounds, sixty five acres of wood and One Hundred Acres of Rich Meadow and Pasturage.

A photographic copy of this detailed auction notice, which covers three pages, was returned from Australia, to Burrswood, Kent, many years ago. It was the gift of the late great grandson of Richard Windeyer,[i] who married Maria Camfield, a daughter of William Camfield, and sister to Henry. Richard and Maria went to New South Wales in 1835, where Richard Windeyer became one of the leaders of the Sydney bar, and a member of the first elected legislative council of New South Wales. Their son Sir Richard William Charles Windeyer became Chief Justice in N.S.W.

There seemed no purpose for William Camfield to remain at Burrswood. His son, William, the brother of Henry, had died in the spring of 1831, and is buried in St John's

(i) The late Sir Victor Windeyer. Retired Judge, from whom a letter was received at Burrswood in July 1987. He died 23rd November 1987.

Churchyard, Groombridge. The stone over his grave bears the words, 'He died unmarried in the 34th year of his life, beloved by all who knew him, 30th May 1831'.

Susannah Matilda Camfield married William Henty at St Nicholas' Church, Brighton, on 18th August 1834. They too went to Australia. Eliza (Bessie) remained with her father who had moved to Brighton, until his death, on 14th July 1850, at the age of 81. Then she too went to Australia and lived with her sisters.

Yet the memory of the house named Burrswood lived on. During Henry Camfield's latter years, and when he suffered moods of despondency, his wife made use of a stratagem which never failed. She would lure him with deft questions to speak of his father and his sisters, and his old beloved home. Returning to his childhood and the years before he had sailed away on the *Caroline*, he would lead his wife through those vanished Elysian fields, and he could forget, for a time, the dissatisfactions of his present life. In a letter dated April 1839, Matilda wrote to her sister Bessie, 'We still spend our Sunday very pleasantly. We get up early and go to Church, and after tea we go to Church again ... such a pretty garden with almost as much fruit in it as there had been at Burrswood, and quite as many nesting birds.[i]

(i) The extracts from letters are taken from *The Henrys - An Australian Tapestry*, Marnie Bassett, 1954.

IN THE

VALE OF GROOMBRIDGE,

KENT.

Particulars

Of the Singularly Beautiful

Freehold Estate,

OF

BURRSWOOD,

Situated in the Celebrated VALE of GROOMBRIDGE, on the North Side of

THE RIVER MEDWAY,

COMPRISING ABOUT

357 ACRES,

Of superior Land, in high cultivation, presenting from a finely undulated surface many delightful Sites for the erection of a Residence suitable to a Domain esteemed for its

Romantic and highly Picturesque Character,

The [illegible] of which possession may be had at Michaelmas next, is within about Three Miles of

TUNBRIDGE WELLS.

The [illegible] in convenient Inclosures along the Bank of the River, including

Sixty [illegible] ACRES OF ORCHARDS AND HOP GROUNDS,

Sixty Five Acres of Wood,

AND

One Hundred Acres of Rich Meadow and Pasturage,

The Timber is very ornamental, Game is abundant; Streams of the finest Water intersect the Property, and there are several Ponds well stocked with Fish.

In addition to many other local advantages, the Estate is entitled to all the privileges of Sir ANDREW JUDD's munificent Scholastic Establishment at Tunbridge.

Which will be Sold by Auction, by

MR. SHUTTLEWORTH,

AT THE AUCTION MART, BARTHOLOMEW-LANE,

Opposite the Bank of England,

On THURSDAY, AUGUST 30, 1832, at Twelve o'Clock.

IN TWO LOTS.

Burrswood *circa* 1835. By courtesy of Mr John M. C. Wheeler, M.B.E., Hon. Curator The David Salomons Collection, who made known the existence of a watercolour of Burrswood in that collection. Grateful thanks are extended to him and to the Centre Manager, Alan Birkett, for permission to borrow a 35mm transparency of this painting.

Sir David Salomons, J.P.

David Salomons became the owner of Burrswood in Kent between 1832 and 1851. The baronetcy was not conferred upon him until 1869. During 1829 he had bought the lease of a small villa, named Broomhill, near Tunbridge Wells. At this time he was thirty-one and his wife, Jeanette, was six years younger. They had no children. Both David Salomons and his wife were members of prosperous families. They had another house in London, as David Salomons worked in the City, and he might have been described as a stockbroker, banker and merchant. His main interest was not business but public life. For this he possessed every attribute except one. He was hindered by one insuperable obstacle as by religion he was a Jew and in the 19th century it was expedient to become a Freeman of the City of London as a preliminary to following any occupation within the boundaries of the City. David Salomons' whole endeavour was directed to bring about toleration between persons of every faith, who were desirous to enter professions hitherto closed to them. This he did. But the long list of official appointments which were accorded to him extend over many years - years during which he won ground very slowly, not by force of words, but through respect for his integrity during the years of opposition. In 1831, the year before he bought Burrswood, David Salomons became a liveryman of the Coopers Company. In 1839, he was appointed, by Queen Victoria, to become High Sheriff of Kent. The Queen had succeeded to the throne two years previously, in 1837, during which year Disraeli had entered parliament, after having made four previous attempts. Although Disraeli had been baptized into the Christian Church, when he was a boy of thirteen, there had been much opposition by those whose minds were closed within their own outlook, and who stood in the way of this man who was the son of a distinguished Jewish father. Disraeli did not become Prime Minister until 1868, but his influence in the government of 1858-59, will have been instrumental in legalising the admission of Jews to Parliament.

But what could have motivated this young and talented man, David Salomons, to buy Burrswood? The question must remain unanswered. The advertisement for the auction draws attention to

> The valuable Estate of Burrswood extending from the Village of Groombridge, along the course of the Medway, parallel to the domain of Lord de la Warr, a peculiarly rich district of a fine picturesque part of the COUNTY OF KENT, and from its contiguity to Tunbridge Wells, and numerous objects of interest, possesses every advantage that can promote domestic enjoyment and yield a pleasant variety of rural life. The Estate lies in the Parishes of Speldhurst and Ashurst, comprising 319 acres and 31 Perches of Rich Arable, Meadow, Pasture, Orchard, Hop, and Wood Land. The present Residence is upon a limited scale, but possesses the requisites for Family convenience. Burrswood was sold for £12,500.

The architect, Decimus Burton, was commissioned to re-build the house, which took four years, between 1834 and 1838. Only the front and the back grey stone walls, and the chimneys, together with the main sitting rooms, remain as part of the building in which the new owner lived, after completion of the new house. Many changes have taken place over the years, especially since 1948. The main staircase, which now curves down into the entrance hall, was unseen formerly, when it descended behind the panelled wall to the former billiard room.

But the distinguishing feature of the house remains outside. Burrswood was re-built to be a Jewish home, and this must be a sacred place and under the protection of Almighty God. God commanded, through Moses, that His word must be written 'upon the door-posts of thy house and upon thy gates'. The Talmudic sages interpreted this command to mean that the Law of God is not actually to be written on the door-posts, but that a mezuzah be fastened to them. This mezuzah is a small sheet of parchment upon which are inscribed by hand two paragraphs of the Law of God which are read by Jews in the shema prayer every morning and evening. The mezuzah reminds us that those who occupy these premises believe that there is only one God in Heaven and upon earth, and of the presence of God within that home.'

There is, another historical reason for the mezuzah. During the long years of persecution of the Jews, there were many times when Jews were homeless; they could only wander from place to place, begging for help. But when the mezuzah was seen fastened to the door of a house, a starving Jew knew he would be sure of a welcome, food and rest. The mezuzah is therefore a symbol of hospitality and brotherly love. The mezuzah must be fastened to the house, and on the right-hand side of the front door, as one enters, and on the outside. The presence of four mezuzah are to be seen at Burrswood. The frontispiece shows the open parchment, in stone, upon the ascending chimney stack, to the right of the main front door. Above the door, but to the right, another may be seen, facing those who might walk up the path from the village. On the south side of the house, there are two further mezuzah in stone. Hebrew lettering is visible, reading from right to left, diagonally, which is a part of the instructions. The consonants form one of the biblical names for God. It is probable that behind the stone scrolls, there are tubes containing a parchment scroll with the relevant texts. Immediately before the mezuzah is fixed into place, the following benediction is said,

> 'Praised be Thou, O Lord, our God, King of the universe, who has sanctified us by Thy commandments, and hast commanded us to fix the mezuzah'.

During the service to consecrate the house a Psalm of David will be said,

> 'Lord, who shall abide in Thy tent? Who shall dwell in Thy holy mountain? He that walketh blamelessly and worketh righteousness, and speaketh truth in his heart....

And the Psalm 101,

> 'I will sing of Thy loving kindness and justice; unto Thee, O Lord, will I sing praises'.

On the wall behind the house, which would have been the south wall of the former billard room, there is an Italian inscription,

AD OGNI UCELLO SUO NIDO E BELLO.

Translated this says, 'to every bird its nest is beautiful'. There is no information why this should be here. Maybe it was a sentiment in remembering a happy occasion during a visit to Italy.

In 1847 David Salomons was admitted an Alderman for the Ward of Cordwainers, and in 1855 he reached the culmination of his career, and became Lord Mayor of London. He accepted a baronetcy in 1869, on the condition that his nephew, David Lionel Salomons should be his heir. His great nephew, Captain David Reginald Salomons gave his life-belt, and so his life, to one of his men when his ship, the *Hythe*, was sunk in collision with another vessel in Mudros Bay, on his way to Gallipoli, with the 1st/3rd Kent Fortress Engineers, in 1915, and so the baronetcy died out.

The following prayer, found in a well-worn manuscript book, with the name of Emma Abigail Salomons inscribed on the front, seems to lead Burrswood into the future.[(i)] Emma Abigail, the daughter of Jacob Montifiore, who was both a pioneer and an owner of land in New South Wales, was also the grandmother of Captain David Salomons.

> Heal us, O Lord, and we shall be healed,
> save us, and we shall be saved,
> for Thou art our praise.
> We beseech Thee to restore our health,
> and grant a perfect cure unto all our diseases;
> for Thee, O God, art a merciful
> and faithful Physician.

The Salomons Crest is a lion and the words DEO ADJUVANTE. - God Assisting.

(i) This prayer is reproduced by courtesy of the Executive Director of the Jewish Welfare Board.

The Cottage *circa* 1646. Renamed St Mary's Cottage 1955. Restored *circa* 1974.

Burrswood gates which formerly opened onto the green, probably date from the second period of smithcraft in England. During World War II cast iron gates and railings were commandeered for armaments; these were apparently not collected. Now at the entrance to East Lodge. *Photograph* M. Filmer.

Drawing of the coach house, harness room and apple store by courtesy of the artist Victor Roberts

Drag used by Sir David Salomons. Drawn by two pairs of horses. By courtesy of Mr H. Middleton, Curator of Maidstone Museum, permission to photograph the coach which is in the Tyrwhitt Drake Museum for Carriages, Maidstone. It is thanks to Mr John Wheeler, (Hon. Curator, The David Salomons Collection) that this carriage was located. *Photograph* John D. Sharp.

Sir Walter George Stirling, Bart, J.P.

Sir Walter George Stirling, Baronet, J.P., became the owner of Burrswood in 1870, until almost the close of the nineteenth century. (i) He was born on 6th September 1839, just ten years after his grandfather, Admiral Sir James Stirling, had become Governor of the West Coast of Australia. Sir Walter Stirling was an Extra Groom in Waiting to Queen Victoria. In 1875 he married Eliza Horatia Frederica, Viscountess Clifden, the widow of the 3rd Viscount Clifden, who had died in 1866. (ii)

Viscountess Clifden was an Extra Lady of the Bedchamber to the Queen. Burrswood, Groombridge, together with a home on the Isle of Wight, are listed as the seats of Sir Walter.(iii) For a short time the full social life of the end of the 19th century was enjoyed at Burrswood. Zealously attended by an unseen and numerous staff, a life style that was taken for granted was to be swept away for ever in less than half a century. Through the eyes of a small child, a relative, who visited Burrswood, the Victorian atmosphere, in a rather unpretentious house, made an unforgettable impression. But the principal attraction was to watch the oxen pulling the plough. The use of oxen was considered out of date and extravagant, but Lady Stirling continued to use them. In spite of entertaining many of the notable people of the time, and visiting Cowes frequently, the Stirlings seem to have been homely people who enjoyed their garden and were

(i) *First Directory of Kent.*

(ii) and (iii) *Burke's Peerage,* 1893.

devoted to their horses. Sir Walter was so attached to one horse that he had a monument erected to him in a field which was called the Memorial Field, or by the local people, the Monument Field. This field lies on the right-hand side of the top drive. By 1948 the plinth was no longer visible. Lady Stirling took a considerable interest in the management of the estate; but Sir Walter caused comment among the villagers by his preference for string in place of boot laces; and he carried a hoe whenever he walked in the gardens, to sever any weed that presented itself before him.

A tomb-stone in the Churchyard of St John the Evangelist, bears the inscription:

Eliza Horatia Frederica Viscountess Clifden V. & A.(i)
Wife of Sir George Stirling Bart, of Burrswood
Born 16th July 1833. Died 22nd April 1896.

Sir George Stirling Bart, of Burrswood
Born 6th September 1839. Died 6th June 1934.

(i) Viscountess Clifden V. & A. The Victoria and Albert Award was a Royal Order first established on 10th February 1862, and available only to women. It was awarded to forty-five women. The death of Prince Albert on 14th December 1861 may have been the reason it ceased.

The Grand Duke Mikhail Nikolaievitch

The Grand Duke Mikhail Nikolaievitch is known to have stayed at Burrswood during 1887.(i) The fourth son of Tzar Nicholas I, he was born on 13th October 1832. On 28th August 1857, he married Olga Feodorovna, formerly Cacilie Auguste, at St Petersburg. She was the youngest daughter of Leopold, Grand Duke of Baden. Their son, Nikolai, born in 1859, was shot during the Russian Revolution, at the Fortress of St Peter and St Paul, in St Petersburg, in 1919. Between 1863 and 1881, the Grand Duke was Tzarist Administrator of the Caucasus region, and commander of the armed forces of the Caucasus Military District. During the Russo-Turkish War of 1877-78, he was commander in chief of the Russian army of the Caucasus. He served as chairman of the State Council between 1881 and 1905, and in that body represented the conservative views of the Russian nobility and bureaucracy. (iii)

There is no direct answer as to why he should have stayed at Burrswood, but there is direct confirmation that he did so. For many years a picture of the Grand Duke could be seen in a school room of the former village school. When a new school was built, the picture did not reappear.(ii) But the memory of the Duke's visit remained for many years, among the villagers of Groombridge, and the happy occasions when the Duke invited the children to tea. It might be assumed

(i) and (ii) *Groombridge Old and New* and *Discovering Groombridge*, Barbara Lee.

(iii) *Modern Encyclopaedia of Russian and Soviet History* vol. 22, 1981. *Burke's Royal Families of the World.*

that the visit was personal; perhaps to visit Princess Alexandra, the eldest daughter of King Christian IX of Denmark, who had married Edward, Prince of Wales, in 1863. Princess Alexandra's sister had been married to Tzar Alexander III, of Russia, in 1866. Sir Walter Stirling, who owned Burrswood at this time, had held an official appointment to H.R.H. Prince Leopold, the father of Olga Feodorovna, therefore it seems reasonable to suppose that he had made his country house available for this visit.

Edwin James Johnstone

Edwin James Johnstone owned Burrswood between 1906 and the time of his death in 1918. Mrs Johnstone remained the owner of the house for a further year, until 1919.[(i)] James Johnstone senior, the father of Edwin James, had been the proprietor of the *Standard* newspaper between 1842 and 1861.[(ii)] Educated at Harrow, Edwin James became Editor of the newspaper between 1872 and 1877. During his years at Burrswood he became the father of five children; one son was educated at Charterhouse, but this was after the family no longer lived at Burrswood. He owned one of the early Wolseley motor cars; he benefitted from many servants, including ten gardeners. Each Sunday he and his family attended a service at St John's Church, Groombridge. One of his little daughters, who died at Burrswood, is buried in the graveyard of the Church. Mrs Johnstone kept a number of griffons which were shown regularly at Crufts. But it is for the gardens that Mr Johnstone will be remembered. His brother, W. A. Johnstone, was a traveller. He brought to Burrswood rare shrubs and plants; he made the gardens as they are today. The plants were transported to Groombridge by train,[(iii)] and taken to Burrswood in cartloads. Vast quantities of daffodils were brought from Holland, and strewn across the fields and copses, where they flourish every spring. Many cultivated varieties were brought as well, and planted in clusters about the gardens. The banyan

(i) *First Directory of Kent*, 1870.

(ii) *Dictionary of National Biography*.

(iii) Groombridge Station was opened in 1866 and closed in 1985.

trees, which grow upwards on the stone walls of the house, on either side of the door which leads to the terrace, were probably his gift. The early part of the 20th century had brought about great social changes in Britain. Industrial capitalists were entering politics, and replacing the great landowners as the dominant class. In like manner these wealthy men were acquiring some of the country houses and living in a way hitherto undreamed of. But Britain was upon the verge of a momentous calamity, such as had never been envisaged. Three times within the century a crisis with Germany had been making an ultimate world war ever more inevitable. King George V had been on the throne for the past two years since 1910.

But here the immediate story of the house of Burrswood should pause for a moment. There is another home [i] which is merging, imperceptibly, with Burrswood. The full significance of this coming together will only be seen in retrospect, when events are retraced, and when 'far back through creeks and inlets making comes silent, flooding in, the main'.[ii] It is Sunday evening, 18th February 1912, and a dark damp night, but as it is close to 9.30 p.m., the great wood fires in Burrswood are dying down for the night. The children are already in bed and the staff have retired for the night. The house will be well lighted, by one of the model electric generators supplied to well-to-do owners of country houses; it may be that Mr and Mrs Johnstone have already mounted the main stairway, by the billiard room, which was unseen on entering the main reception hall.

But the other home is a very small house, built onto the pavement, with three steps up to the front door, and a basement. The house stands on the crest of a steep hill; on

(i) 204 Milkwood Road, Herne Hill, London.

(ii) Arthur Hugh Clough, 1819-61.

either side are many identical houses, side by side from the bottom of the hill, or continuing further up the long drab road. Behind the houses is a railway line, walled off from the small gardens. Frequent trains pass, belching black smoke, which lingers in the still, damp air. The street is poorly lit by incandescent gas burners on tall stands, which had been lighted by a lamplighter, earlier in the evening, and which will be extinguished towards morning by the same man, who will pull a chain hanging from the high lamp. But on this damp Sunday evening people can be discerned, emerging through the darkness, and very quietly entering the house, shutting the door immediately to prevent the cold air entering an unheated hall. The door of the room, on the right, just inside the hall, is open, and here these people stand, and watch in wonder; they are immediately embraced by a peace and a stillness for which they are unprepared. They know that a young woman is dying tonight. They have known her for years. But the face of the dying woman is radiant with a beautiful smile. A glorious light is about her, and beside her, holding her hand, her mother is singing, quietly muting a warm coloratura voice to the smallness of the room; she is singing a hymn of faith, in the presence of the nearness of death ... [(i)]

And now the narrative returns to Burrswood.

On Tuesday, 20th February, the *Evening Standard* will surely have been delivered to Mr Johnstone; and on Wednesday, 21st February, he will have received many newspapers including the *Standard* whose reporter would have been among the many journalists directed to the little house, at 204 Milkwood Road, Herne Hill, London, to report upon events which had taken place, in the room of the young woman who had been dying.

(i) 'The Rock that is higher than I', adapted from the 61st psalm by Mrs Kerin's father, William Price Wilson.

A quarter of a century later the memory of one reporter was still crystal clear when he wrote -

> In those days I was a young reporter on the Standard Newspapers, a company owning the *Standard*, a London morning newspaper with great political traditions, and the *Evening Standard*. Pre-war London was as prosperous as it was irreligious; when news came that a young girl living in one of its suburbs had experienced miraculous healing by angelic intervention, every newspaper and every news agency of importance must have sent a reporter down to South London, to investigate the phenomenon.[i]

There seems every probability that the story of the instantaneous healing of Dorothy Kerin was read in Burrswood, in 1912. She herself did not come to the house for another thirty-six years!

On the 4th August 1914, the Prime Minister of the last Liberal[ii] Government in Britain, Mr Asquith, announced that the country was at war with Germany.

Mr Johnstone made part of Burrswood available to the Red Cross. The most seriously wounded soldiers were brought by ambulance, along the path which leads from the green. He himself joined the Labour Corps.[iii] As technology advanced, single seater planes, and later two seater planes,[iv] crossed and recrossed over the sky above Burrswood, from

(i) Healing in His Wings, A. J. Russell, 1937.

(ii) 1905-15.

(iii) The Labour Corps formed that part of the British Expeditionary Force responsible for the manual labour of digging trenches etc. for the army. It was a multi-national corps, instituted in 1914, that finally numbered about 25,000 men.

(iv) Sopwiths and Bristols. During World War I Sopwith aircraft were in greater number than any other aircraft. Sir Thomas Sopwith who died 27th January 1989, made his maiden flight in a Sopwith plane in 1910. His foresight in 1935 produced the Hurricane, the renowned fighter aircraft that, with the Spitfire, saved this country in the 1940 Battle of Britain.

some of the eight aerodromes which were constructed in Kent. Many of the pilots were still almost boys, straight from school, who had received their training in a matter of hours, before being sent on missions, in which they were both pilot and gunner.
The armistice was signed on 11th November 1918. Burrswood suffered no structural damage.
Mrs Johnstone moved from Burrswood in 1919, just a year after the death of her husband and the house remained untenanted for the next eight years.

Sir Derrick William Inglefield Watson

Sir Derrick William Inglefield Watson, 4th Earl of Earnock, Co Lanark, came to Burrswood in 1927. He owned the estate until 1948, but only actually lived at Burrswood until 1937, when it was offered for sale, together with either 97, 248 or 600 acres of land. [(i)]

Sir Derrick had succeeded his brother, the 3rd Earl, who had been killed in action, in 1918.[(ii)]

His seat is spelt Burrs Wood, Old Groombridge, Kent, in Burke's Peerage and Baronetage. He was a Captain of the 4th Battalion, Queen's Own Royal West Kent Regiment, T.A., C. C. Kent 1931-37. He had been educated at Eton and Christ Church, Oxford.

On 15th April 1925, he was married to Margrett Georgina, daughter of Col. T. Robertson-Aitman, C.B. of the Ross. They had a baby son when they came to Groombridge, and their daughter was born at Burrswood on 13th February 1931. Sir Derrick Watson's father had developed the Hamilton coal mines, and had built the Lanarkshire railway in order to transport the coal from his mines. The Hamilton mines were closed after the second world war. Sir Derrick will be especially remembered for his Clydesdale horses. A personal memory of Sir Derrick comes from one who was a village boy, in his teens, during the years he was living at Burrswood. [(iii)]

He remembers that Sir Derrick attended St John's

(i) *Country Life*, 16.10.1937.

(ii) *Burke's Peerage and Baronetage.*

(iii) Letter 1987.

Church, on the green. He was very friendly with the vicar and was regarded by the village folk as their squire. Once a year Sir Derrick brought a cricket eleven to play the village team on the Groombridge pitch. This was considered a great social occasion and also once a year Sir Derrick had an open day at Burrswood, to which everyone went, with especial interest in seeing his flowering shrubs and the gardens. The entrance at the East Lodge was still being used; formerly the rhododendron drive this was kept entirely weedless by the small boys of the village who were guaranteed the sum of one half-penny, for every weed they could find, as they walked to the farm to obtain milk.

The year 1937 was not an auspicious time to advertise a large country house. The house remained empty when Sir Derrick moved away. This was a critical time when another war seemed inevitable, and yet every political effort was being made to avert it. The ever increasing problem to find adequate staff, together with the memory of air raids towards the latter years of World War I, made country dwelling, in a rural area, no longer tenable. The former days of English country life could not be reclaimed.

In 1938 Germany annexed Austria. Then Hitler's troops invaded Czechoslovakia. When Germany entered Poland the moment had come to declare war. World War II lasted until Germany surrendered in 1945. Burrswood was requisitioned by the Army, and became the headquarters of the Royal Ordnance Corps. The surrounding woods were used for ammunition dumps.

During the years of war, and the passing and repassing of enemy aircraft above the house, no structural damage was done to the house, beyond the loss of glass in the windows on one occasion, when a bomb was dropped in the woods below the second lawn. The glass was restored to the windows the following day.

When the last of the army vehicles had vacated Burrswood,

the house stood empty for two years. Wholly unkempt within, and the paths dilapidated by the wheels of vehicles carrying heavy equipment over years, the weeds and the undergrowth grew swiftly, entirely unchecked. But the nightingales came again to the woods and the little furry creatures which multiply under unswept leaves knew freedom from the footsteps of men, and every day the sun rose in the east and dipped towards evening behind the hills to the west, so that an afterglow, of colours which are often not of this world, would cover the land with the glory of golden light. And silence came again to Burrswood except for a quiet breeze in the top-most branches of the trees so like the sound of the sea.

By Order of Dr. S. C. Ghose.

KENT AND SUSSEX BORDER

Amidst unspoilt country, commanding distant Southerly Views, convenient for the old world Village of Groombridge, some 4 miles west of Tunbridge Wells.

HIGHLY SUITABLE FOR A SCHOOL, NURSING HOME, COUNTRY CLUB, etc.

Particulars and Conditions of Sale of

The Charming, Stone Built Country House of Regency Design

known as

Groombridge Manor

(formerly BURRSWOOD)

NEAR TUNBRIDGE WELLS

9 Principal Bed and Dressing Rooms, 10 Secondary and Staff Bedrooms, 5 Bathrooms, Lounge Hall, 5–6 Reception Rooms, Excellent Domestic Offices with twin "Aga" Cookers. Double Garage and Stabling for 4.

MAIN ELECTRICITY, PRIVATE WATER SUPPLY, SEPTIC TANK DRAINAGE, GARDEN and GROUNDS, INCLUDING PADDOCKS and WOODLANDS OF APPROXIMATELY 29 ACRES.

POSSESSION ON COMPLETION OF PURCHASE of the House and about 20 Acres

which Messrs.

IBBETT, MOSELY, CARD & CO.,

incorporating E. J. CARTER, BANKS & BENNETT (*Established* 1797)

are instructed to offer FOR SALE BY AUCTION (unless previously sold by Private Treaty) at

The Castle Hotel, Tunbridge Wells,

on FRIDAY, 31st OCTOBER, 1947, at 3 p.m.

Burrswood – southern aspect. 1948

Dorothy Kerin

Miss Dorothy Kerin bought Burrswood from Sir Derrick Watson on the 21st April 1948. The house was blessed in September 1948 at the time of the Festival of St Michael and All Angels. A little chapel was dedicated at the same time. This was a small room, which might well have been the butler's pantry in former times. The Bishop of St Albans, the Right Reverend Philip Loyd,[(i)] dedicated both the house, and the chapel, to St Michael. Bishop Sawa, of the Serbian Church, was present, and there were many guests.

The auction notice which had been prepared for the sale of the property, to take place on Friday, 31st October 1947, at the Castle Hotel, Tunbridge Wells, stated that Groombridge Manor, formerly known as Burrswood, near Tunbridge Wells, on the Kent and Sussex border, amidst unspoilt country, commanding distant southerly views, convenient for the old world village of Groombridge, some four miles west of Tunbridge Wells, was highly suitable for a school, nursing home, or country club. Possession to be on completion of the purchase of the house, together with about twenty acres of land.

The two auction notices, 1832 and 1947, are studies in the social changes of the 19th and 20th centuries. It was not now practicable to advertise a large country house 'with superior land in high cultivation presenting from a finely undulated surface many delightful Sites for the erection of a . . . Domain esteemed for its . . . highly Picturesque Character'.

(i) Bishop of St Albans 1945-50. Formerly Bishop of Nasik.

Two world wars had come between these notices prepared for sale by auction. After World War I, and two decades later, the World War II, the oldest form of employment for women was no longer attractive. Domestic labour, with its longstanding memories of drudgery and exploitation, remained unpopular, even though the National Institute of Houseworkers had been established in 1948, to raise its prestige. The home life of England had changed radically. The estate agent had tried to dissuade Dorothy Kerin, a single woman, with no apparent means, from becoming the owner of a house which would need unprecedented repairs, and an adequate staff to maintain it. Dorothy Kerin went to view the house, for the first time, on a day of torrential rain. Her car was driven across the village green, from the Crown Inn, through the entrance to Burrswood. Just inside, on the left-hand side, she would have passed the South Lodge.(i) This had been the home of the bailiff in former days.

The car made its way very slowly along the ascending, winding lane. The path was furrowed and deep ruts were unpredictable, after the many years of heavy military equipment which had passed this way. After almost three-quarters of a mile of difficult ascent, the path being flooded in many places by overflowing spring water and uninhibited vegetation, the long grey stone wall of the kitchen garden would have been passed on the right-hand side, and the first habitation would have been seen. This was the first building upon the land - a tenanted cottage converted from two smaller dwellings and referred to in the auction notices as 'the cottage' .

Just beyond this the high grass slope, surmounted by a grey stone building, heralded the courtyard of stables, the coach house and harness room. Behind this, and behind the stables,

(i) Restored in 1979 and renamed Burrswood Lodge.

but not seen immediately stood the wash house, with its tall chimney, that can still be seen today. Finally the car would have been driven through a further gateway, marked Burrswood.

Let Dorothy Kerin tell, in her own words, of the moment when she saw the house for the first time through this relentless rain; a gaunt relic of mid-nineteenth century architecture, surrounded by a saturated overgrowth of weeds,

> As soon as I arrived on the door-step I felt sure this was the house, and found it answered exactly to the description of the house in my mother's dream, just before she died. (i) I turned to the friend who was with me, saying, 'there is no need to look further; this is the house'. It was dilapidated and almost as derelict as Chapel House had been, (ii) but I seemed to see it as it could be - something beautiful for God to use. The property had been chopped up, and odd bits sold, including the two farms and cottages. But in my mind's eye I visualised it all complete again.

On the other side of the lane, opposite to the house, she would have seen a high grass bank, surmounted by massive pine trees, which were in alignment with ley lines, (iii) and from under which a spring flows out several miles beyond the surrounding fields. These pine trees are no longer there. Just one remains, two gaunt arms, reaching upwards and inter-twined, denuded of their bark. Their demise was mainly due to the drought in 1977, and not to the storm in October 1987.

(i) *Fulfilling*, Dorothy Kerin, 1952. Mrs Emily Jenny Kerin 1862-1943.

(ii) Chapel House, Ealing. The story is told in *Fulfilling*, Dorothy Kerin, 1952.

(iii) Lines termed 'leys' which are believed to mark pre-historic pathways along which flow currents of energy.

Dorothy devoted the first nine years at Burrswood to repairing and re-constructing the house, and to remaking the gardens.(i) The last five years of her life, 1958-63, was a time of continous building, as well as making many visits overseas in response to the invitations which were coming to her. The account of these missions is told elsewhere.(ii) The name of Burrswood became known again about the world, as a home of welcome, to which people turn in their times of perplexity or distress.

In parenthesis, Dorothy still owned Chapel House, Ealing, and seven adjacent houses, in 1948. This property had been requisitioned by Middlesex County Council, but no payment had been received. Indeed no payment was made until 1950. Yet Dorothy Kerin was never in debt. During her years of ceaseless activity she had implicit faith that where God guides, He provides. And she had already been asked to repair and make habitable, two derelict houses, Chapel House, Ealing, in 1930, and Etherton Hill, Speldhurst, in 1946; but first and foremost must come the assurance that God had indeed guided, and that in no way had her own wishes come within her decisions. Then came two further principles; first a perfect, unquestioning obedience to His will and, in her own words, Dorothy explains exactly what she means by this:

> You may well ask how are we to learn obedience? The obedience that brings us to the knowing of God's will for us? To this I so humbly reply, that we must first learn obedience by faithfully doing what is set before us in our every-day lives. In doing whatsoever our hand findeth to do, with all our heart, mind and strength, as unto the

(i) Credit for the restoration of the gardens is entirely due to Mr Frank Hammerton, head gardener 1948-79.

(ii) *Dorothy Kerin: Called by Christ to Heal*, Dorothy M. Arnold. Hodder & Stoughton, 1963.

> Lord. In so doing we shall find that when we have learned to obey in small things, the Lord will ask more intimate and costly obedience from us, and we shall delight in the glory of obedience which is better than sacrifice.[(i)]

Secondly the final principle of her life, but by no means the least, was that she should waste nothing. 'If I were even to waste a piece of orange peel' she said, on one occasion, 'I could expect nothing more to come to me'. Orange peel was saved and made into marmalade.

On the 8th July 1951, Bishop Philip Loyd wrote to Dorothy: [(ii)]

> ... you are constantly in my thoughts and prayers, and I wish I could do more to help you. But it is you whom God has called to Burrswood, and to whom He has given it all, in order that you may give it all back to Him. And if He is to use your offering, as He wants to use it, (and the salvation of so many souls, old and young depend upon it) then it must be a costly offering, which the Beloved has stamped with His own Cross. So we who love you dearly must needs leave you to make your own offering in the way that God has appointed for you. God bless you.

In 1954 Dorothy wrote a letter to the Burrswood International Fellowship, which included these words:

Surely the most exciting and wonderful adventure in life is when we put our hand in God's Hand, and trust Him utterly, for indeed His ways are not our ways, and His ways are best.

(i) Words spoken by Miss Kerin which are recorded in her own voice.

(ii) Since 1929, Bishop Philip Loyd had been a staunch friend and counsellor to Dorothy. He died in 1952, just six months after writing this letter. A memorial tablet to him is in the Oratory, Burrswood (formerly the Chapel of St Luke).

Chapel of St Winifred, Court Lodge. Dedicated by the Bishop of Chichester on 2nd May 1956.

The Window - *The Healing of the Daughter of Jairus* - was previously blessed at the dedication of Chapel House, Ealing on 25th October 1930.

St Luke's Chapel, Burrswood 1957. The window, *St Luke*, had been dedicated at Chapel House, Ealing on 10th May 1934.

The former rose garden, Burrswood.

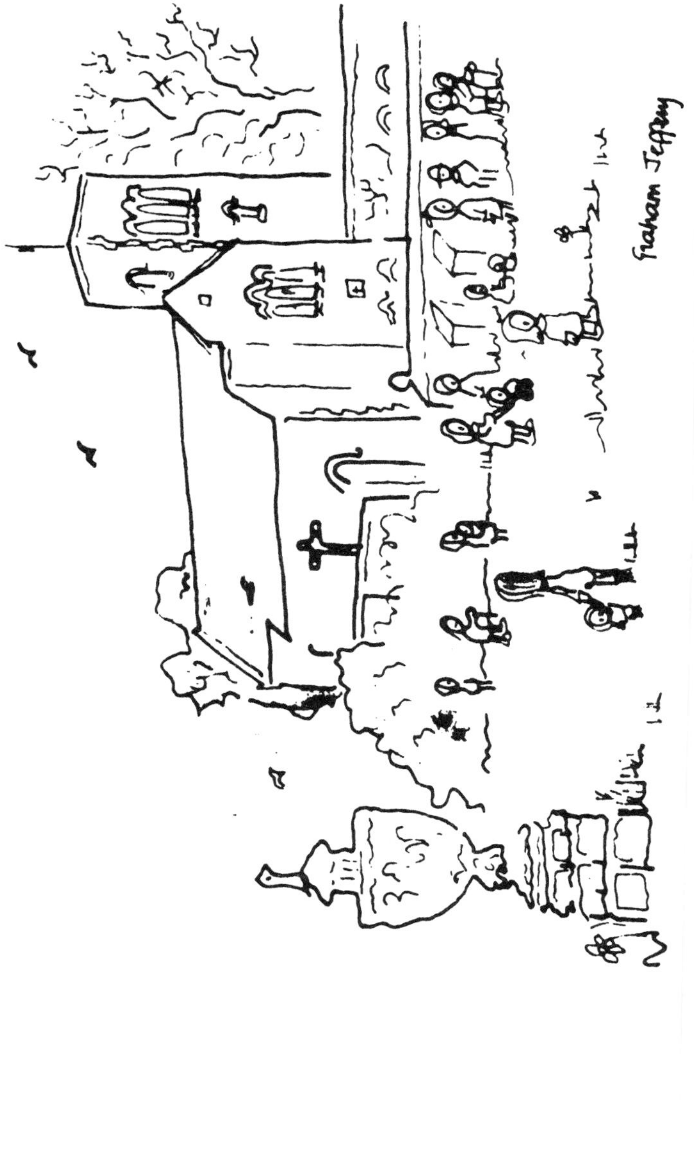

The Church of Christ the Healer 1960. By courtesy The Revd Graham Jefferey

During the spring of 1959 Dorothy Kerin was given a vision. She was praying in the early morning, when ... let her own words speak,

> I saw in the rose garden here a church; there it stood in all its strength and beauty. Out of the windows there streamed a golden light, lighting up everything it touched. As I watched, I noticed that this light came from within. Then I heard the Voice that I had learned to know, saying, 'Build this Church for Me'.The foundation stone was laid on the 29th September 1959. On the 10th October 1959, Dorothy wrote a letter to the Burrswood Fellowship:Humbly I believe He has asked me to build this Church for Him, and I know our efforts will be blessed and used by God, in the spreading of His glorious Ministry of Healing. The healing of body, mind and spirit, that our stricken, suffering and agonising world is in such need of today.

On 14th May 1960, the Church was dedicated to Christ the Healer. It was entirely free from debt, yet no money had ever been asked for it. The countries which had sent gifts were represented for many years by numerous small flags around the font.

It was a day of brilliant sunshine, in spite of a very poor weather forecast. Every seat in the Church was occupied, and many people sat on the steps outside and along the terrace. Loud speakers connected them with the Church service. Everyone was given a service booklet of eight pages and the whole service was tape recorded. On page 2 the Foundress prays the Bishop to consecrate the Church in these words: 'Reverend Father in God, we pray you to consecrate our Church.' And the Bishop makes reply, 'I am ready to proceed to the dedication'. Then on page 7 the supreme consecration is given for which all have been waiting; the congregation kneels as the Bishop stands at the High Altar, that beautiful 17th Century altar which came from the private chapel of an Italian family who could trace their descent from the 9th century. Placing his hands upon the altar the Bishop clearly and with solemn emphasis pronounces the blessing. As he stresses all that the altar would mean in the sacramental life of this Church he pauses between each of the three important words to make the sign of the cross above it.

> Vouchsafe, O Lord our God, to **bless** - **hallow** - and **consecrate** this Altar to Thine honour, and for the perpetual Memorial of the one Oblation once offered upon the Cross; through Jesus Christ our Lord, Who liveth and reigneth with Thee and the Holy Spirit, one God, world without end.
>
> Amen.

When the prayers for this house of God were completed, the Altar was vested, and even as this happened a fanfare of trumpets rang through the Church, out onto the terrace and through the sunlit gardens to reverberate across the valley to the far hills and beyond.

* * *

The following dates give some indication of the initial buildings which were bought by Miss Kerin, and the buildings which she herself had added to the property between 1948 and 1963:

Burrswood 1948-57

Burrswood - House	Sale completed 21st April 1948
Stone Court Farm and Home Farm	Tenancy from 31st May 1955
The Cottage(St Mary's)	Tenancy from May 1955

ORDER OF SERVICE

FOR

THE CONSECRATION OF

THE CHURCH OF CHRIST THE HEALER

BURRSWOOD

by

THE LORD BISHOP OF COVENTRY
THE RIGHT REVEREND CUTHBERT BARDSLEY

THE LORD BISHOP OF LEWES
THE RIGHT REVEREND J. H. L. MORRELL

and

THE DEAN OF GUERNSEY
THE VERY REVEREND E. L. FOSSARD

on

Saturday, 14th May, at 2.30 p.m.

GEORGE THALBEN-BALL D.mus.

and

THE TEMPLE CHOIR

Trumpeters: **ROYAL MILITARY SCHOOL OF MUSIC KNELLER HALL**

Interior of the Church of Christ the Healer 1960.

Dorothy Kerin. This photograph was taken, without her knowledge, during a service in 1960.

Entrance to the extension that connects St Michael's - the Nursing Home - with the Church. Formerly a covered way. 1987. *Photograph* M. Filmer.

First cottage built by Miss Kerin (The Nest)		1952
The Bungalows 1 and 2		1955
New Cow house (to accommodate 20 cows)		1950
Court Lodge, Ashurst Hill	Bought by Miss Kerin	1955
	Resold	1959

Burrswood 1957-63

1957-58	The east wing of the main house, which had consisted of rooms for the servants of former ownersof Burrswood, together with the high wall which occluded a view of the gardens, was demolished, to make way for the new building for guests - St Faiths .	
1957	18th February. Chapel of St Luke dedicated.	
	17th July. Foundation stone laid for St Faith's.	
1958	New circular staircase descending into main reception hall, constructed to accommodate extension to St Luke's Chapel.	
1958	15th February.	St Faith's dedicated.
	25th March.	Chapel House, Speldhurst, was closed.
	5th May.	Extension to St Luke's Chapel blessed.
1959	18th February.	Chapel House dedicated. Chapel within Chapel House dedicated.
1959	29th September.	Foundation stone laid for the Church of Christ the Healer.
1960	14th May.	The Church of Christ the Healer was dedicated.
1961	18th February.	The Chaplain's House dedicated.
	29th November.	Dedication of Little Sweden &

The Haven. The name Little Sweden is to remember that the wood with which this log house is constructed was the gift of the people of Sweden in thanksgiving.

1962 7th June. St Luke's House blessed.

1963 After the death of Miss Kerin:
19th June. New wing to The Haven blessed. The drives to Burrswood reconstructed. This had been under contract before the death of Dorothy Kerin, but the heavy snow of 1962/63 delayed the work. The pathways to the house of Burrswood had never been repaired.

* * *

Chapels associated with Burrswood

1946 Chapel of the Good Shepherd consecrated at Speldhurst, by the Bishop of St Albans, The Right Reverend Philip Loyd.
This Chapel had been a Red Cross hut used in World War II.

1948 Moved to Burrswood - stood on terrace. Known as the children's chapel.

1982 Restored by The Dorothy Kerin Trust.

* * *

1948 A further chapel consecrated in the garden of Etherton Hill (Chapel House) Speldhurst. It has remained there.

* * *

1948 Chapel dedicated to St Michael, during dedication of the house of Burrswood to St Michael and All Angels. This Chapel was used for the first services for healing, with the laying on of hands, on Thursdays. Later became staff sitting room; then TV room. Into this room came the first pictures of the landing on the moon, 1968. Latterly a kitchen.

1955 St Winifred's, Court Lodge, Groombridge. Dedicated by Lord Bishop of Coventry. In 1959 the chapel was dismantled when the house changed hands. The memorial window was transferred to the Church of Christ the Healer, 1960. The dog was added to the window.

1957 The Chapel of Christ the Healer, Guernsey, dedicated by the Lord Bishop of Winchester on 9th May. The story of this Chapel is told in *Thy Son Liveth*, by the Revd Frank Drake. Published by Hodder & Stoughton Ltd., 1959.

* * *

1957 Chapel of St Luke, Burrswood. Dedicated by Bishop Cuthbert Bardsley, Lord Bishop of Coventry, and Bishop Warden to Burrswood since 1954.

1958 Enlargement to Chapel (St Luke's) blessed by Lord Bishop of Coventry.

1960 The furnishings of this chapel were placed in the original Lady Chapel in the Church of Christ the Healer and much of the space converted into two rooms for patients. The Altar remained and the smaller chapel is now known as The Oratory.

1960 14th May. The Church of Christ the Healer dedicated and the High Altar consecrated by The Rt Revd Cuthbert Bardsley, Lord Bishop of Coventry. The Lady Chapel dedicated by The Rt Revd J. H. L. Morrell, Suffragan Bishop of Lewes.

* * *

Towards the end of her extended life-span of fifty years, it seemed right to Dorothy Kerin that she should bear witness yet again to her miraculous healing and to the personal encounter with Our Blessed Lord Himself. But this time she was able to avail herself of the modern technology which was not known in 1912. Dorothy left a full account of her healing in her own speaking voice.(i) She has left to those who come after her a full account of all that took place on Sunday night, the 18th February 1912, at 204 Milkwood Road, Herne Hill, London.

> Many years ago I had a personal encounter with our Living Lord. By this I mean that I met Him face to face. He laid His hand upon my life and restored me to perfect whole ness in the twinkling of an eye. My healing was instantaneous and complete. There was no moment of weakness or convalescence, and this after five years of so called hopeless illness. During this time I had been bed-ridden, suffering from general tuberculosis and other complications. The last of twenty-eight doctors had said that nothing more could be done to help me, and we must expect death, which was inevitable. Everything that love and skill could do had been done, and now the end was expected at any moment. There had been weeks of semi-consciousness during which time all efforts to prolong life had been abandoned. A little company of friends and relatives were gathered around my bed waiting for the last flicker of life to depart, when some of them saw a great light over the bed. They first thought it was Jesus taking this little spirit to Himself, but as they watched they saw this little emaciated form raised to a sitting position by unseen hands. She opened her eyes and began to speak, and this is what she said, 'Do you hear, I am well. I must get up and walk.'

(i) This recording, in the voice of Miss Kerin, was made at her request, during the early part of the 1960s, in her room, called The Dorothy Kerin Room, Chapel House, Burrswood. It was spoken in the presence of Miss Marisa Filmer, and Dorothy M. Arnold author of *Dorothy Kerin: Called by Christ to Heal,* Hodder & Stoughton, 1964.

No, they did not hear, but as they watched they saw her who was dying, get out of bed and stand before them, every whit whole, every whit whole. And this in the twinkling of an eye. Jesus had touched her. She was healed.

There are two significant things concerning this miraculous healing. The first is had it been any other voice than the voice of the Living Lord, nothing would nor could have happened. Secondly, the servant to whom the Lord spoke knew it was the Lord, and obeyed without hesitation or question, and so this miracle happened.

It is noteworthy that during the period of unconsciousness I was oblivious to the suffering that was endured by those who watched over and tended me. For me it was a time of indescribable joy and bliss in a place and environment of exquisite harmony. I seemed to be going somewhere with a definite purpose, when suddenly I was aware of a lovely form clad in dazzling white, He was coming towards me. And I knew it was Jesus. He said, 'Dorothy, will you go back and do something for Me'. To which I answered, 'Yes, Lord'. Then it was I was commanded to get up and walk.

Our Lady appeared to Dorothy on the night of Sunday, the 11th March 1912. Dorothy was staying in the home of Dr Edwin L. Ash. [(i)] She tells of being awakened out of sleep by a voice saying, 'Dorothy'. She continues,

I sat up and saw at the foot of my bed a wonderful light, out of which came the face of a beautiful woman, holding a lily. She came very near to me, and said, 'Dorothy, you are quite well now. God has brought you back to use you for a great and privileged work. In your prayers and faith many sick shall you heal; comfort the sorrowing and give faith to the faithless. Many rebuffs shall you have, but

(i) *Faith and Suggestion*, Dr Edwin L. Ash, 1912.

> remember you are thrice blessed; His grace is sufficient for thee. He will never leave thee.'(i)

On the 18th January 1940, twenty-eight years later, the Archbishop of Canterbury (ii) gave his patronage to the healing ministry which was her response to Our Lord's commission.

Returning from time to time into her inmost self, to live again through each moment of direct encounter with Our Lord, in His Glory,(iii) must surely have enabled Dorothy to maintain her perfect obedience, even when, to quote her words:

> boilers burst, structural repairs were necessary, and it seemed as if there was little else that could happen. That was a wonderful time for trusting God, as it were, in the dark. And I was reminded often, in those days, of His promise, 'I will never leave thee'.

At another time she wrote,

> Continuing to have faith was hard work. Those were the days when one went on, not daring to do anything except just trust in God, and leave it all to Him. In those days of testing we learned to trust Him, and the faith that He had given us turned into knowledge.

Dorothy came to Burrswood just thirty-six years after the healing, and the request, and her own response, which was to give her life-span a further fifty years.

The first seventeen years might well be called a wilderness period. She had become an invalid as a child of thirteen years of age; now she found herself in her twenty-third year re-entering a world to which she was a stranger. It was a

(i) *The Living Touch*, Dorothy Kerin, first published 1914, latest edition 2008
(ii) Cosmo Gordon Lang, Archbishop of Canterbury 1920-42.
(iii) *The Living Touch,* Dorothy Kerin, first published 1914, latest edition 2008

time of unrest - militancy and a country on the brink of war. A world in which a woman had no personal voice. But even greater than her immediate problems, of which poverty was no small part, there was the total lack of understanding, indeed ridicule and incredulity, which oppressed her. Yet she must pray without ceasing, first that God would tell her why she had been healed, and then she must pray without ceasing that she might be purified, indeed that her own freewill should be annihilated that she might become what God wished her to become, in order that she might fulfil His trust in her, and accomplish His plan through her.

There were times when she was afforded the deeper spiritual mysteries [(i)] yet these moments were accompanied by the consequential agony of the experience. For many months she suffered the Sacred Dereliction [(ii)] and subsequently the Wounds of His Holy Passion.

After this preliminary time of seventeen years, there came a further test over nineteen years, as she took the responsibility of several houses in which to shelter those who came to her for healing. Therefore when Dorothy Kerin came to Burrswood there remained fourteen years before her. By this time obedience had become so central to her life that she might never, for any personal reason of disinclination or fatigue, refuse to see any person(s) who asked to see her. Many came without an appointment, but to all she extended the same welcome, walking towards the visitor and taking both hands into her own. For those thus privileged there remained a memory, not of a person, but of a reflected Light that shone through the eyes of Dorothy, a glimpse of the Divine Compassion which touched the centre of each person's need.

Death came swiftly and unexpectedly to Dorothy. On

(i) *Dorothy Kerin: Called by Christ to Heal,* Dorothy M. Arnold, 1964.
(ii) *The Teaching of Dorothy Kerin*, J. Ernest, 1977.

Friday evening, the 25th January 1963, as she settled for sleep, Dorothy was heard to say,

The irrevocable pattern of the Lord is fulfilled. I love Him - I love Him - I love Him.

The following morning, Saturday the 26th January, she was in her room, in Chapel House, Burrswood, speaking with the resident physician about the business affairs of Burrswood, and while she was yet speaking she died.[i]

It was a morning with a clear blue sky, from which the sun shone upon the dazzling whiteness of fields and woodland, frozen under three weeks of intermittent coverings of snow, and which crowned the hills in golden light.

Miss Kerin was born on Thursday, 28th November 1889, at 6 Boyson Road, Walworth, London.[ii] When her death took place on that Saturday, 26th January 1963, at Burrswood, she was already in her seventy-fourth year. On the 18th February 1963 a service in memory of her was held in the Church of St Martin-in-the-Fields, London at which the Lord Bishop of Coventry gave the address. This took place just one year to the day after a service of thanksgiving had been celebrated, in the same church, for the fifty years which had followed her miraculous healing on 18th February 1912.

The Public Trustee accepted the charge of Burrswood between 1963-69 and the Dorothy Kerin Trust came into being on 3rd June 1963.

The Trust Deed affirms that the trust, known as the Dorothy Kerin Trust since its inauguration is empowered to receive (without distinction of race, colour or nationality) patients at the nursing home of Burrswood;

(i) Dr Edward Aubert. The account of the weeks which preceeded the death of Miss Kerin recorded in *The Life of Dorothy Kerin*, 1983, and *Dorothy Kerin 1889-1963,* 1987.

(ii) *The Life of Dorothy Kerin,* Johanna Ernest, 1983.

to arrange for the holding of services according to the rites of the Church of England at the Church at Burrswood, known as the Church of Christ the Healer. . . and for that purpose to pay or contribute to the stipend of a Clerk in Holy Orders duly authorised to conduct such services by the Bishop of Rochester.

On Thursday the 31st January 1963, the funeral service for Miss Kerin took place in the Church of Christ the Healer. The committal followed in the Churchyard of St John the Evangelist, Groombridge, to await her reinterment in the chancel of the Church that she had built, as soon as the business matters caused by her death, had been adjusted.

The diary of the day, kept at Burrswood, records,
12 o'clock service arranged by Bishop West and the Chaplain.
The Bishop of Rochester read lesson;
The Bishop of Tonbridge said prayers;
The Bishop of Coventry gave sermon.
The Church was full - chairs and standing.
The committal was in St John's awaiting transference to the Chancel of Christ the Healer. [(i)]

(i) This still awaits to be honoured. A Petition has been signed and the legal formalities have been complied with.

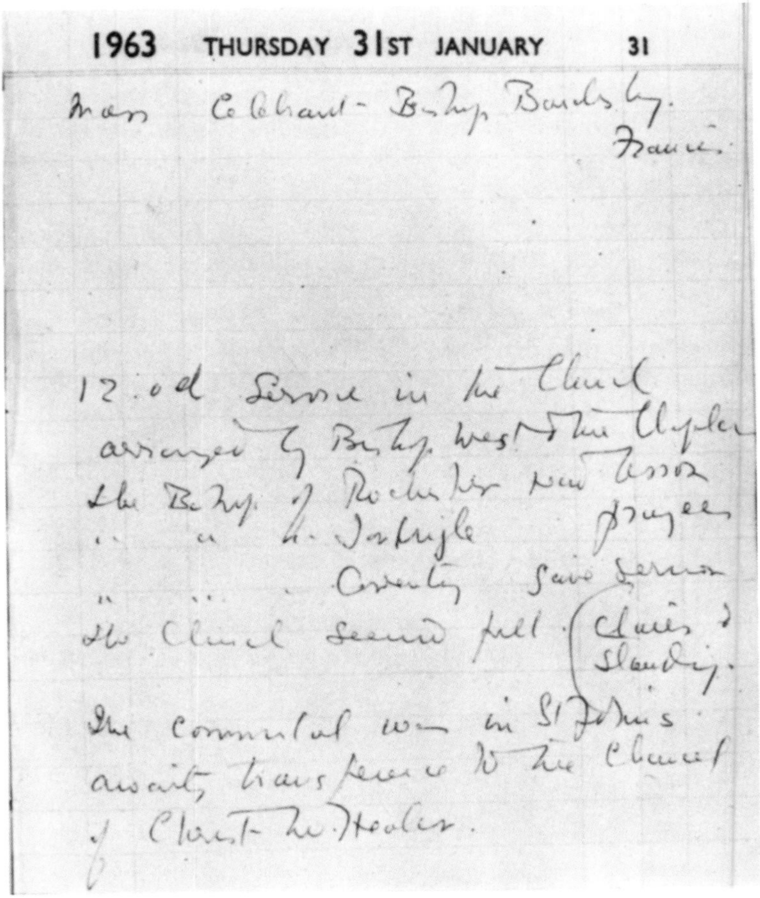
1963 THURSDAY 31ST JANUARY 31

Mass Celebrant - Bishop [illegible]
France.

12.0 clock Service in the Church
arranged by Bishop West & the Chaplain
the Bishop of Rochester read lesson
" " the [illegible] prayers
" " " Coventry gave sermon
the Church seemed full (chairs & standing).
The committal was in St John's
awaiting transference to the Chancel
of Christ the Healer.

Burrswood Diary for 31st January 1963. The funeral service for Dorothy Kerin is recorded - and 'the committal was in St John's awaiting transference to the chancel of Christ the Healer'.

Appendix

1965 The Breakthrough Cross on the roof of the Lady Chapel was sculpted out of scrap metal by Ophelia Gordon-Bell. This was blessed on the 23rd November 1965.

1980 On St Peter's Day, 29th June 1980, the hydrotherapy pool was blessed at Burrswood and dedicated to St Peter, having been formally opened by the Marquess of Abergavenny who kindly consented to become the first Patron. A plaque on the eastern wall within the building states:

> This Plaque is erected in memory of our Founder, Dorothy Kerin, whose Memorial Fund has contributed to the children's play room (now Bocky's Kitchen) and swimming pool (hydrotherapy pool).
>
> 'Suffer little children to come unto Me'

Additional Building

Early 1950s Wellspring (formerly Temple Cottage)

1962 St Lukes (Physician's House)

1963 The Colt House (Maria Preston, the original Matron at Burrswood, supported the cost of this project and lived in the property until approximately 1998)

2006	Colt House divided to form two self contained flats
1960s	Swedish Log House and Little Sweden (amalgamated into one in 1996)
1970	Kalulu
1981	Building of St David's as a home for its architect, Mr Elidir Davies, who married Kathleen Burke-Collis, Governess to Dorothy Kerin's children. Converted to Conference Centre in 1996
1987	St Michael's extension was due to be opened on 18th October, two days after the great storm. Due to extensive roof damage, the opening was postponed by a month
1994	Extension of The Nest to provide two-storey accommodation
1996	The 'Forward In Care' project was launched in 1996, resulting in:
1996/97	Phase I Link corridor to St Peter's Outpatient department, accommodating Counselling rooms, Physiotherapy Treatment area, Medical Consulting Room, new changing rooms and Reception area. Opened by Sir Maurice Laing on Fellowship Day, 4th July 1997. Architect Mr David Christmas
1998	Phase II Complete upgrade of Chapel House, guest

	house. Re-dedicated by Bishop Morris Maddocks on 11th July 1998. Architect Mr Mark Eddison
1998-2000	Phase III Re-building of St Faith's to provide 19 ensuite patient rooms. Officially opened by HRH Princess Alexandra on 17th May 2001. Architect: Mr Mark Eddison (MEBP partnership)
1999-2000	Extension of St David's Conference Centre, re-opened on 9th March 2000 by Michael Toynbee, DL
2002	Phase IV Extension to the Lady Chapel to provide a semi-circular Apse. Re-dedicated by Bishop John Perry on Fellowship Day, 13th July 2002
2002	Re-negotiation of the farm lease reincorporated Home Farm Cottage (built in the 1930's). This, together with a pair of semi-detached Victorian cottages on the periphery of the estate were sold in 2006/7 to provide capital funding for the conversion of Chapel House
2008	Phase V Conversion of Chapel House to provide additional individual ensuite patient rooms and relocation of guest accommodation. At the time of reprinting, work is still in progress.

Architects involved with Burrswood

Decimus Burton FRIBA	Original house 1834- 1838
Philip Beauchamp FRIBA	1952 onwards
Elidir Davies FRIBA	Original building of St David's 1977-1988
R Walker FRIBA	Wellspring
David Christmas FRIBA	Forward In Care Phase 1
Mark Eddison (MEBP Partnership)	Forward In Care Phases 2, 3, 4, 5

Builders

Russell Bros (Groombridge) Ltd	1948-84
Nicholas Butcher (Penshurst)	1985-88
Baxall Construction Ltd	1996-1998
Barwick Construction Ltd	1998-2000
H J Johnston Ltd	2008-

Bibliographical Notes

Ash, Edwin Lancelot *Faith and Suggestion* (Herbert & Daniel, London, 1912.)

Arnold, D. M. *Dorothy Kerin:* Called by Christ to *Heal* (Hodder & Stoughton, London, 1964.)

Bassett, Marnie *The Hentys: An Australian Tapestry* (Oxford University Press, 1954.)

Davidson Ross,J. *Dorothy: A Portrait* (Hodder & Stoughton, London, 1958.)

Drake, Frank *Thy Son Liveth* (Hodder & Stoughton, London, 1959.)

Ernest, J. R. M. *The Church of Christ the Healer* (The Dorothy Kerin Trust, 1972.)
The Teaching of Dorothy Kerin (The Dorothy Kerin Trust, 1977.)
The Life of Dorothy Kerin (The Dorothy Kerin Trust, 1983.)
Dorothy Kerin 1889-1963, *Her Ministry of Healing,* 1987.

Farr, R. *Will You Go Back?* (The Dorothy Kerin Trust, 1970, re-printed 2008)

Hyamson, A. M. The Salomons

Jerrold,Clare *Picturesque Sussex* (Valentine and Sons Ltd, The Shire Series.)

Kerin, Dorothy *The Living Touch*, 1st published, 1914. *Fulfilling,* 1st published 1952. Both re-printed 2008

Lee, B. *Groombridge Old and New*

	Groombridge Place
	Discovering Groombridge
	St John's Church, Groombridge.
Mackinnon, D.	*History of Speldhurst.*
Parkes, James	*The Three David Salomons at Broomhill* (T. A. Constable Ltd.)
Russell, A. J.	*Healing in His Wings* (Methuen and Co. Ltd., 1937.)
Screeton, Paul	*Quicksilver Heritage* (Thorsons Publishers Ltd., 1974.)
Stacy Waddy, R. P.	*Philip Loyd Missionary and Bishop* (Mowbrays 1954.)
Trevelyan, G. M.	*History of England* (Longman, 1972.)

Index